DRACULA

In the spring of 1875, Jonathan Harker travels to Transylvania on a business visit to the home of Count Dracula. Jonathan does not really want to go because in a few months' time he is getting married to his beautiful Mina, and he does not want to leave her.

While he is staying in Castle Dracula, he keeps a diary. And every day he has more and more terrible things to write. Why does he see Count Dracula only at night? Why can't he see the Count in the mirror? And who are the three beautiful women with their red mouths and long sharp teeth that come to his room at night?

At home in England, Mina is staying with her friend Lucy in a town by the sea. She waits for Jonathan's letters, but they do not come, and Mina is afraid. Perhaps Jonathan is ill or in danger …

Mina is not afraid for herself, of course, or for her friend Lucy. What danger can there possibly be for two young women in a quiet English seaside town?

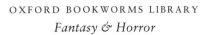

OXFORD BOOKWORMS LIBRARY
Fantasy & Horror

Dracula

Stage 2 (700 headwords)

Series Editor: Jennifer Bassett
Founder Editor: Tricia Hedge
Activities Editors: Jennifer Bassett and Alison Baxter

American Edition: Daphne Mackey, University of Washington

BRAM STOKER

Dracula

Retold by
Diane Mowat

OXFORD UNIVERSITY PRESS

OXFORD
UNIVERSITY PRESS

Great Clarendon Street, Oxford OX2 6DP

Oxford University Press is a department of the University of Oxford.
It furthers the University's objective of excellence in research, scholarship,
and education by publishing worldwide in

Oxford New York

Auckland Cape Town Dar es Salaam Hong Kong Karachi
Kuala Lumpur Madrid Melbourne Mexico City Nairobi
New Delhi Shanghai Taipei Toronto

With offices in

Argentina Austria Brazil Chile Czech Republic France Greece
Guatemala Hungary Italy Japan Poland Portugal Singapore
South Korea Switzerland Thailand Turkey Ukraine Vietnam

OXFORD and OXFORD ENGLISH are registered trade marks of
Oxford University Press in the UK and in certain other countries

ISBN 978 0 19 4237499

Typeset by Wyvern Typesetting Ltd. Bristol

Printed in Hong Kong

ACKNOWLEDGEMENTS
Illustrated by: Paul Fisher Johnson

CONTENTS

JONATHAN HARKER'S DIARY

I

Count Dracula

My story begins about seven years ago, in 1875. My name is Jonathan Harker, and I live and work in London. My job is to buy and sell houses for other people. One day a letter arrived for me from a very rich man who lived in Transylvania. He wanted to buy a house in England, and he needed my help. The man was Count Dracula, and I agreed to help him.

I found a house for him, and he asked me to take all the papers for it to Transylvania. I was not very pleased about this. I was planning to get married in the autumn, and I did not want to leave my beautiful Mina.

"But you must go, Jonathan," she said. "The Count is rich, and perhaps he will give you more work later."

So I agreed to go. I did not know then of the terrible danger which waited for me in Transylvania.

And so, on May 4th I arrived at a little town called Bistritz. Transylvania was a strange and beautiful country. There were mountains, trees, and rivers everywhere. And somewhere high in the mountains was the Count's home, Castle Dracula. I had six hours to wait before the coach came to take me there, so I went into a little hotel. Inside the hotel it was warm and friendly. The people there were all laughing and talking. "Where are you going?" they asked me.

"To Castle Dracula," I replied.

Suddenly the room was silent, and everyone turned to look at me. I could not understand why they all looked afraid.

"Don't go there," someone said.

"But I have to," I answered. "It's business."

They began to talk again, but they were no longer laughing. Slowly, the hotel keeper's wife took the gold cross from her neck and put it into my hand. "Take this," she said. "There is danger at Castle Dracula. Perhaps this will help you."

When the coach arrived and I got into it, a crowd of people came to watch, and I heard the word "vampire."

The coach traveled up into the mountains. Higher and higher it went, faster and faster. The sun was bright, but above the trees there was snow on the mountain tops. Then suddenly

the sun went down behind the mountains, and everywhere was dark. In the forest around us, the wolves were howling. It was a terrible sound.

Suddenly the coach stopped. A small carriage came down the narrow road on the right. Four black horses were pulling it, and the driver was dressed in black, with a black hat pulled down over his face.

"Where's the Englishman?" he called. "I've come from Castle Dracula!"

He looked strange, standing there in the moonlight, and suddenly I was afraid. But it was too late. I could not go back now.

Soon we were on our way to Castle Dracula. The mountains were all around us, and the moon was behind black clouds.

A small carriage came down the narrow road on the right.

I could see nothing—but I could still hear the wolves. The horses went faster and faster, and the driver laughed wildly.

Suddenly the carriage stopped. I opened the door and got out. At once the carriage drove away, and I was alone in front of the dark, silent castle. I stood there, looking up at it, and slowly the big wooden door opened. A tall man stood in front of me. His hair was white, and he was dressed in black from head to foot.

"Come in, Mr. Harker," he said. "I am Count Dracula." He held out his hand, and I took it. It was as cold as ice!

Slowly, the big wooden door opened.

I went into the castle, and the Count carefully locked the door behind me. He put the key into his pocket and turned to go upstairs. I followed him, and we came to a room where a wood fire burned brightly. In front of it there was a little table with food and drink on it. The Count asked me to sit down and eat, but he did not eat with me. Later, we sat and talked by the fire. His English was very good, and while we talked, I had time to look at him carefully. His face was very white, his ears were like the ears of a cat, and his teeth were strong like the teeth of an animal. There was hair on his hands, and his fingers were very long. When he touched me, I was afraid.

It was nearly morning when I went to bed, and outside the wolves were still howling.

The next morning I found my breakfast on the little table in front of the fire. Now that it was light, I could see that Castle Dracula was old and dirty. I saw no servants all that day.

The Count did not come to breakfast, but there was a letter from him on the table.

"Go anywhere in the castle," it said, "but some of the rooms are locked. Do not try to go into these rooms."

When the Count came back in the evening, he wanted to know all about his new house in England.

"Well," I began, "it's a very big house, old and dark, with a high wall all around it. There are trees everywhere. That's why the house is dark. It has a little church too." And I showed him some pictures of it.

He was pleased about the church. "Ah," he said, "so I shall be near the dead."

We talked for a long time, and once I fell asleep. I woke up suddenly and found the Count's face near me. The smell which came from him was terrible. It was the smell of death.

"You're tired," the Count said. "Go to bed now." And when he smiled, his face was the face of a wolf.

Our business was now finished. The Count had all the papers for his new house, and there was nothing to keep me in Transylvania or in Castle Dracula, but the Count did not want me to leave. I was alone with him in the castle, but I never saw him in the daytime. I only saw him at night when he came and sat with me. We always talked until the morning, and he asked me many questions about England. "I have plans to go there myself soon," he said. "Tell me about sending things to England by ship." So we talked about ships and the sea, and I thought about Mina, and her friend Lucy. Lucy and her mother were staying by the sea, and Mina was planning to visit them there some time. Stupidly, I told the Count about them.

There was no mirror in my bedroom, but I had one with me, a present from Mina. One morning I was standing in front of it, and I was shaving. Suddenly a hand touched me, and a voice said, "Good morning." The Count was standing next to me. He was standing next to me, *but I could not see him in the mirror!*

My hand shook, and I cut myself. Blood began to run down my face, and I saw that Count Dracula was watching it hungrily. Suddenly he put out his hand. He had a wild look in his eyes, and I was afraid. But his hand touched the gold cross at my neck, and his face changed. He took the mirror from me, went to the window, and a minute later the mirror was lying in a thousand pieces far below. He did not speak, but left the room quickly. And I stood there and asked myself *why* I could not see this man in the mirror.

The Count's hand touched the gold cross at my neck.

I went over to the window and looked out. I was high above the ground. Many of the doors in the castle were locked. Suddenly, I understood. I was a prisoner!

2

I Am in Danger

One evening the Count said, "You must write to your London office and tell Mr. Hawkin that you'll be here for another month."

When I heard this, I went cold. Another month! But what could I do? I worked for Mr. Hawkin, and the Count's business was important to him, so if the Count needed me, then I had to stay. I wrote my letter, but I knew that the Count planned to read it. I could not tell Mr. Hawkin that I was a prisoner in Castle Dracula!

That evening the Count did not stay and talk with me, but before he left the room, he turned to me and said, "My young friend, sleep only in this room or your bedroom. You must never fall asleep in any other room in the castle. You will be in danger if you do."

When he left, I went to my room, but I could not rest and began to walk around the castle. Many of the doors were locked, but I found one which was open. I pushed back the door and saw that there was a window in the room. It was a beautiful night, and the mountains looked wonderful in the soft yellow light of the moon. Suddenly, something moved below me. It was the Count. Slowly, he came out of the window—first those hands, like the hands of an animal, and then his head. He began to move down the wall, *head first*. With his black cloak around him, he looked like a horrible black bird—and my blood ran cold. What *was* Count Dracula?

I shivered and sat down for a minute. The room was warm and friendly. I think that many years ago it was a room for the ladies of the castle, and I decided not to go back to my cold, dark room, but to sleep in this room. So I lay down and closed my eyes.

Suddenly I felt that I was not alone. In the moonlight from

the window I saw three beautiful young women. They were watching me and talking quietly. "He is young and strong," one of them said.

"Yes. There are kisses for all of us," another answered.

I was excited and afraid. I knew that I wanted those soft red mouths to touch me.

One of the women came nearer. Her strong white teeth touched my neck. I closed my eyes and waited. "Kiss me! Kiss me!" I thought.

Suddenly there was a cry of anger. It was the Count! He pulled the woman away from me, and her bright blue eyes

The Count pulled the woman away from me.

turned red with a wild anger. I looked at the Count, and his eyes were burning with all the fires of hell.

"Get off him!" he cried. "He's not for you! Stay away from him." A second later, the women were no longer there. They did not leave by the door, but they were no longer there!

I remember no more of that night. When I woke up, I was in bed in my room. My gold cross lay on the table next to me, bright in the morning sun.

I knew then that those women were vampires and that they wanted my blood.

Two nights later, the Count came to me. "Write to Mina," he said. "Tell her that your work in Transylvania is finished and that you are coming home."

How pleased I was when I heard this! But then the Count said, "Say that you are at Bistritz, and put June 29th on the letter."

I shivered when he said this. I knew then that the Count planned to kill me on that day. What could I do? There was nothing. I could only wait and try to escape. But the Count took away all my other clothes and my travel papers, and he locked the door of my room.

A week or two later, I heard noises in the castle, the sound of men working. "Perhaps one of them will take a letter out of the castle for me," I thought.

But it was too late! It was already June 29th, and that evening from my window I saw the Count leave the castle, with my letter to Mina in his hand. He was going to mail it! I knew that

I had to do something before it was too late.

Vampires can only come out at night, so I knew that there was no danger during the day. The next morning I decided to visit the Count's room to see what I could find. To do this I had to get into it by the window. This was possible because his room was just below my bedroom, and there were little holes in the wall between the stones. I could put my feet in these, and I could use the heavy curtains from my window to hold onto. It was dangerous, but I had to try.

Slowly I moved down the wall. Once or twice I almost fell, but at last I found myself in the Count's bedroom.

The room was empty. The Count was not there. I looked for the castle keys, but I could not find them. Over in one corner of the room there was some gold, and on the other side of the room there was a big wooden door. It was open, and I saw that there were some stairs going down. I went down them, and I came to another door. This was open too, and I found myself in a room with a stone floor. Slowly, I looked around me. There were about fifty wooden boxes in the room. They were coffins, and they were full of earth. In one of them lay the Count! I could not say if he was dead or asleep. His eyes were open and looked cold and stony, but his face did not look like the face of a dead man. His lips were still very red, but he did not move. Slowly I went nearer. I thought perhaps that he had the castle keys on him. But when I looked at those cold, stony eyes, my blood ran cold. Afraid, I turned and ran back to the window. I did not stop to think until I was back in my room.

That night the Count came to me again. "Tomorrow you

In one of the coffins lay the Count.

will return to England," he said—and I knew that tomorrow was the day of my death.

I lay down on my bed, but I did not sleep very well. During the night I heard women's voices outside my door and then the Count, saying, "Wait. Your time has not yet come. Tomorrow night—you can have him then." The women laughed, a low, sweet sound, and I shook with fear.

Morning came at last, and I was still alive. "I must escape," I thought. But first I had to get the keys.

Once again, I went down the wall and into the Count's room. I ran down the stairs to the room with the coffins.

The Count was there, in his coffin, but he looked younger, and his hair was no longer white. There was blood on his mouth, which ran down across his neck. My hands were shaking, but I had to touch him to look for the keys. I felt all over his body, but they weren't there. Suddenly I wanted to kill Count Dracula. I took a workman's hammer and began to bring it down hard on to that horrible, smiling face. But just then the head turned, and the Count's burning eyes looked at me. His bloody mouth smiled more horribly than ever. I dropped the hammer and stood there shaking. What could I do now?

Just then I heard the sound of voices. The workmen were coming back. I hurried back up the stairs to the Count's room. Below, I heard the noise of a key. The workmen were opening a door. So there was another door to the outside down there! I listened carefully and heard the sound of hammers. They were getting the coffins ready for a journey—perhaps to England! I remembered the Count's words about his plans to visit my country.

I turned to run back downstairs to find this open door. But I was too late. A cold wind ran through the castle, and with a crash the door at the top of the stairs closed and locked itself. I could not get back down the stairs.

Soon I saw from the window the heavy carts full of coffins,

I saw from the window the heavy carts full of coffins.

and the workmen drove away. I was alone in the castle with those terrible vampire women.

While I was writing these words in my diary, I decided what to do. I must try to escape. I will try to get down the wall outside. The window is high above the ground, but I have to try. I will take some of the gold with me—if I escape, perhaps it will be helpful later.

If I die, it will be better than the death that waits for me here. Goodbye, Mina! Will I ever see you again?

3

Lucy in Danger

While Jonathan was away, I was very unhappy. He did not write to me often, and when he did, his letters were strange and very short. I knew that something was wrong. But what? Was Jonathan in danger? I thought about him all the time. Why didn't he come back to England and to me?

I felt better when at last I did get a letter from him. Jonathan said that he was coming home and was at Bistritz. But again it was a short, strange letter. "Perhaps he's ill," I thought.

My friend, Lucy, also wrote to me. "I know that you will be happy for me," she wrote. "Arthur has asked me to marry him! Isn't it wonderful? I love him very much. He's away just now, and you know that Mother and I are staying at Whitby, by the sea. Please come and stay with us, and I can tell you all about it."

Arthur Holmwood loved Lucy very much. I was really pleased to hear her news, and I decided to go immediately. It would help me not to think about Jonathan all the time.

Lucy met me at the station, and it was wonderful to see her again. She was full of life and talked happily of her plans. "Oh, Mina," she said to me. "I am really happy. I love Arthur very much."

But sometimes it was hard for me, because when Lucy talked of Arthur, I thought of Jonathan again.

The weather was good, and Lucy and I walked a lot, sometimes by the sea, but we often went up to the old church on the hill.

At night, Lucy and I slept in one room, but sometimes she walked in her sleep. She began to sleep badly, and her mother and I decided to lock the bedroom door at night.

Then one day the weather changed. The sky was black and heavy, and that night there was a terrible storm. Lucy was very excited by it, and she sat by the window all night and watched the sea.

The next morning there was a ship on the beach.

"It's a Russian ship, from Varna on the Black Sea," Lucy's servant told us. "There are coffins on it, and they're full of earth. And a big black dog jumped off the ship and ran up the hill!"

"And is everyone on the ship alive?" Lucy asked.

"That's the strange thing about it," the servant replied. "There was no one on the ship, either dead or alive."

Everybody in the town was very excited by this strange ship, but there were no answers to the mystery. And nobody saw the big black dog again.

That night I woke up and found that the bedroom door was open and Lucy was not there. I looked for her everywhere in the house, but I could not find her. "I'm afraid for her, I don't know why," I said to her mother.

I knew that Lucy sometimes liked to go and sit quietly in the churchyard, so I hurried out into the night to look for her. And I found her. She was sitting in the churchyard, white in the moonlight, and I thought I saw something dark behind her—something dark and horrible. Slowly, its head moved nearer to Lucy. Afraid, I called out, "Lucy! Lucy!" A white face and burning red eyes looked up at me—and then, nothing! Lucy was alone, asleep in the moonlight. I woke her up, and she gave a little cry. She put her hands to her neck, and I saw that there were two little drops of blood there.

Lucy was sitting in the churchyard, white in the moonlight.

After that night Lucy was worse. She left her bed every night, and her lovely face was white. I was afraid for her and locked the door at night. And I still did not hear from Jonathan. I was unhappy and did not sleep well myself, so one night I went for a walk alone. "Lucy will be all right," I thought. "The door is locked. She can't get out, and no one can get in." But when I came back, I found Lucy by the open window. "Lucy!" I cried. But she did not reply. She was asleep, and near her, just outside the open window, there was something black, like a big bird.

A day or two later, I had a letter. Jonathan was ill and in a hospital in Budapest. "Of course, I must go to him immediately," I said to Lucy. I did not want to leave her, but Jonathan was everything to me. "He needs me," I said.

And when at last I arrived in Budapest and held Jonathan in my arms, I felt happy. Jonathan was very ill, but he was getting better every day. He did not want to talk about his time in Castle Dracula, but he gave me his diary to read. And so I learned about Count Dracula and Jonathan's terrible adventure in the castle. But he escaped! And when he became ill in the mountains, some workmen found him and took him to the hospital. Poor Jonathan! His face was white and thin, and he was still very afraid, but now we were together again, and everything was all right.

Jonathan and I were married on September 1st, and we began our journey home. We arrived back in England on September 18th, and it was wonderful to be home again. Everyone looked happy on that warm autumn evening when we drove through the streets of London. Jonathan smiled and said softly, "Oh Mina, I love you."

"I love you, too, Jonathan," I replied. I was truly happy.

And then, suddenly, Jonathan's face went white, and he cried out. He was looking at a carriage, outside a shop. In it there was a pretty girl with dark hair. She was waiting for someone. And near the carriage, watching the pretty girl, there was a man—a tall, thin man, with long white teeth and a very red mouth. "It's the Count!" Jonathan cried. "Here in London!"

"It's the Count!" Jonathan cried. "Here in London!"

Jonathan put his head in his hands and said nothing for the rest of the journey. I was very afraid for him. Was it really true—that this horrible Count Dracula was here in London?

When we arrived home, there was a letter from Arthur Holmwood. Lucy was dead! My dearest Lucy, dead! It could not be true!

Later we read the letter again.

"Soon after you left," Arthur wrote, "Lucy began to get worse. I did not know what to do. I knew only that I must do something quickly, so I asked our old friend, Jack Seward, to come and see her. "He's a doctor," I thought. "Perhaps he can do something to help Lucy." He came at once, but in the end nobody could help poor Lucy, and she died yesterday.'

JACK SEWARD'S STORY

Lucy's Death

When I heard from Arthur the terrible news of Lucy's strange illness, I went to her immediately. I could see that she was very ill. She lay in bed all day and did not move. She was as white as a ghost, and she was very thin. When night came, she was afraid to sleep, and in the morning, on her neck there were two strange little wounds.

I did not know what was wrong with Lucy. She was losing

blood. But how? Was it through these two little wounds in her neck?

I decided to send for my old teacher Professor Van Helsing from Holland. Perhaps he could help.

He came immediately, and when he saw how ill Lucy was, he said, "We must give her blood at once."

"She can have my blood!" cried Arthur. "All of it—to the last drop!"

Van Helsing was right. With Arthur's blood in her, Lucy began to get better immediately. But before he left, Van Helsing did one more thing. He brought some flowers with a very strong smell, and he put a circle of them around Lucy's neck. "My dear," he said, "these are garlic flowers. Do not take them from your neck tonight, and do not open your window."

Van Helsing had to return to Holland for a few days, and before he left, he told us: "You must watch Lucy every night and be sure that she wears the garlic flowers."

Lucy's mother was ill herself—her heart was not strong— and Arthur had to go back home because his father was dying. So for a week I watched over Lucy myself at night, and sometimes, when I sat by her bed, I heard strange noises at the window. Perhaps it was a tree, or the wind, I thought.

I was working at my hospital during the day, and after a week I was very tired, so one night I did not go to Lucy's house. I needed to sleep, and I knew that Lucy's mother and the servants were there. Also, Van Helsing sent new garlic flowers every day, for Lucy to wear at night.

The next morning at the hospital I had a note from Van

Van Helsing put a circle of garlic flowers around Lucy's neck.

Helsing. "Watch Lucy carefully tonight," he wrote. "I will be with you tomorrow." But that was now today! The note was too late!

I did not wait for breakfast, but hurried to the house immediately. I knocked on the door, but there was no answer. Just then Van Helsing arrived.

"What happened?" he cried. "Did you not get my note? Quick! Perhaps we are already too late!"

We knocked again, but there was still no answer. We went

around to the back of the house, Van Helsing broke the kitchen window, and we went in.

It was dark in the kitchen, but we could see the bodies of the four servants on the floor. They were not dead, but asleep. "Someone put something in their drinks," said Van Helsing. "Come! We must find Lucy if we are not too late!"

We ran up to Lucy's room and stopped outside it. With white faces and shaking hands, we opened the door softly and went into the room.

How can I describe what we saw? The bodies of two women—Lucy and her mother—lay on the bed. The faces of both women were white, and on the mother's face there was a look of terrible fear. In her hand she held the flowers from Lucy's neck, and on the floor there was glass from the broken window.

Van Helsing looked down at the two women. "The poor mother is dead," he said. "But for Lucy it is not too late! Go and wake up the servants!"

I ran downstairs to wake them up. "Put her in a hot bath," Van Helsing said.

After a time, Lucy began to show some life, and they took her and put her in a warm bed. From time to time she slept, but she did not fight to stay alive. She could not eat anything, and she was very weak. We sent for Arthur, and when he came, he was very unhappy. His father was now dead, and he could see that Lucy was very, very ill. One of us sat with Lucy all the time, and that night Arthur and Van Helsing slept in the sitting-room, while I watched over Lucy.

When Van Helsing came back up to me at six o'clock, Arthur was still asleep downstairs. Van Helsing went over to Lucy and looked at her. "The wounds on her neck have gone," he said. "She will soon be dead. Bring Arthur."

When Arthur and I came back, Lucy opened her lovely eyes. "Oh, Arthur," she said softly. "Kiss me, my love."

He moved his head nearer to her, but Van Helsing pulled him back. "No!" he cried. For a minute, Lucy's face was hard and angry. She opened her mouth, and her teeth looked very

"Oh, Arthur," Lucy said softly. "Kiss me, my love."

long and sharp. Then her eyes closed, and she slept. Soon she woke up again, took Van Helsing's hand, and said softly, "My true friend." And then, quietly, Lucy died.

"She's gone," said Van Helsing, and Arthur put his head in his hands and cried.

Later, I went back into Lucy's room, and Van Helsing and I looked down together at her beautiful face.

"Poor girl," I said. "It is the end."

"No," he replied. "This is only the beginning."

Some days later there were strange stories in the newspapers, stories about young children who went out at night and did not go home until the next morning. And when they did go home, they talked about a "beautiful lady." All these children had drops of blood and two little wounds on their necks.

Van Helsing read these stories, and he brought the paper around to me. "What do you think of that?" he asked.

"I don't know," I said. "These two little wounds sound like poor Lucy's wounds, but how can that be?"

Then Van Helsing explained. At first I could not believe it, and we talked for a long time. At last I said, "Are you saying that poor Lucy was killed by a vampire, and that now the vampire is taking blood from these children too?"

"No," Van Helsing replied. "You haven't understood. The vampire which is taking blood from these children is ... Lucy herself."

I was very angry. "That's not true!" I cried.

"Then come with me," he said. "And I will show you."

So that night he took me to Lucy's tomb. He had the key, and we went inside. I was very afraid. In the dark, with the dead flowers lying on Lucy's coffin, the tomb was a terrible place. Slowly, Van Helsing began to open the coffin. Then he turned to me, and said, "Look."

I came nearer and looked. The coffin was empty.

For me, it was a terrible surprise, but Van Helsing only shook his head. "Now we must wait outside," he said.

We waited all night. I was cold and afraid, and I was angry with myself and with Van Helsing. Then, suddenly, something white moved in the trees near the tomb. We went nearer, and we found a little child on the ground, by the tomb. Van Helsing held it out to me, and I looked at its neck. "There are no wounds on the child's neck," I said.

"No," Van Helsing replied. "We are just in time."

The next day, Van Helsing and I went back into the tomb again and opened the lid of the coffin. This time Lucy's body lay there. She died more than a week ago—but she did not look dead. Her mouth was red, and her face was more beautiful than ever. Then Van Helsing pulled back her mouth and showed me her long, sharp teeth.

"Now do you believe me?" he said. "Lucy is now one of the Un-Dead, and with these teeth she will soon kill one of these poor little children. We must stop her before she does." He stopped for a minute and thought. "But we must send for Arthur. He, too, must see—and believe this."

Arthur was very unhappy and also angry. He could not

believe that Lucy was now one of the Un-Dead, but in the end he agreed to come with us to the tomb.

It was just before midnight when we got to the churchyard. The night was dark, but now and then, a little moonlight came through the clouds. Van Helsing opened the door of the tomb, and we all went in.

"Now, Jack," he said to me, "you were with me yesterday afternoon. Was Miss Lucy's body in that coffin then?"

"It was," I replied.

Slowly, Van Helsing opened the coffin. Arthur's face was white when he moved nearer. We all looked down. The coffin was empty!

For a minute, no one spoke. Then Van Helsing said, "Now we must go outside and wait."

Slowly, Van Helsing opened the coffin.

It was good to be outside again, away from the dark, smelly tomb. We stood and waited in silence. Then, through the trees, we saw something white. It was moving nearer to us. Its face was white, its mouth was red, and drops of blood fell from it. Suddenly it saw us and stopped. It gave us a look of terrible anger, and Arthur gave a little cry. "It's Lucy!"

She smiled. "Oh, Arthur, come to me. Leave those others, and come to me, my love," she said sweetly.

Arthur took his hands from his face and opened his arms to her. She was moving nearer to him when Van Helsing ran between them and held out his little gold cross. Lucy stopped and stood back from it. Then, with a look of terrible anger on her face, she went to the tomb and through the door. *The door was closed, but she went through it!*

"Now, Arthur, my friend," Van Helsing said, "do you understand?"

Arthur put his face in his hands and cried, "I do! Oh, I do!"

The next day, Arthur, Van Helsing, and I went back to the tomb. Van Helsing had a bag with him, and when we were in the tomb, he again opened Lucy's coffin. The body lay there, horribly beautiful. Arthur was white, and he was shaking. "Is this really Lucy?" he asked.

"It is, and it is not. But wait, and you will see the real Lucy again," Van Helsing replied.

He took from his bag a long piece of wood and a hammer. Arthur and I stood silent and watched. Then Van Helsing said to Arthur, "You loved Lucy. You must bring her back to us. You must take this piece of wood in your left hand and the hammer in your right hand. Then you must drive the wood through Lucy's heart. It isn't easy for you, but it will soon be done. Can you do this for her?"

"I can," Arthur replied strongly.

His face was very pale, but he held the piece of wood over Lucy's heart and brought the hammer down hard.

Arthur held the piece of wood over Lucy's heart
and brought the hammer down hard.

The body turned from side to side, and a horrible scream came from the open red mouth. Arthur did not stop. Harder and harder he hit the wood with the hammer until, at last, the body stopped moving and lay quiet.

The hammer fell from Arthur's hand, and he stood there, white and shaking. Van Helsing went over to him. "And now you may kiss her," he said. "See! The vampire is dead, and the real Lucy has come back."

It was true. Lucy's face was pale and still, but it was now quiet and restful. Arthur kissed her softly on the mouth, and then Van Helsing closed the coffin again, this time, for ever.

"Now, my friends," Van Helsing said, "we have only just begun. We must find the vampire that killed Miss Lucy. It will be difficult and dangerous. Will you help me?"

"Yes," we said. "We will."

JONATHAN HARKER'S DIARY

Mina in Danger

Some days after Mina got the letter from Arthur, with the news of Lucy's death, she had another letter. This was from Professor Van Helsing, a friend of Arthur's. In it he wrote, "I know from your letters to Lucy that you were her dearest friend. I would very much like to meet you, to talk

Mina had another letter from Professor Van Helsing.

about the time when you were with Lucy at Whitby."

So the Professor came to see us at our house, and we learned the full story of poor Lucy's terrible death. Then Mina gave Van Helsing my diary to read, and he learned about my time at Castle Dracula. He was very excited.

"Ah!" he cried. "Now I begin to understand so many things! This Count Dracula—he was the vampire that killed poor Miss Lucy. Will you help us to find him?"

Of course, Mina and I agreed to help. When I saw Count Dracula in London, I was very afraid, but now I felt stronger because I had work to do.

We began at once. Mina went to stay with Jack Seward at his house, to tell him and Arthur all about the Count, and I went to Whitby. I wanted to find out about the coffins that were in the ship on the night of the storm—the ship that brought Count Dracula to England. After many questions, I learned that the coffins were now in the Count's house in London.

I hurried back to London and to Jack Seward's house. When I told Van Helsing this news, he called us all together and said, "Now the danger begins. I have learned a lot about vampires from old books, and I know that they can come out only at night. During the day they are like dead bodies and must have a place to hide. I think that Count Dracula uses his coffins for his daytime hiding-places. If we can find him in a coffin, we can kill him. Let's go to his house tonight. We'll put holy bread in the coffins, and then the Count cannot get back into them. He'll then have no place to hide during the day, and he will be weaker and easier to fight when we find him."

So that night Van Helsing, Jack, Arthur, and I went out together to the Count's house. Mina, of course, did not come with us. I was afraid to leave her alone, but she said that there was more danger for us than for her.

Jack had some old keys with him, and with one of these we got into the house. It was old and dirty, and the smell of blood was everywhere. We walked through the cold, empty rooms, and at last we found the coffins.

From his bag Van Helsing took some holy bread. "We must put a piece of this in each coffin," he said.

We worked hard. It took a long time to break open each coffin and put holy bread inside. We were just opening the last coffin when Van Helsing gave a cry. "We are too late! The Count is coming!"

We looked up from our work and saw Count Dracula. He came through the dark room like a black cloud. His angry face was white, and his eyes burned like red fires. Van Helsing held out his gold cross, and the Count stopped. Afraid for our lives, we ran from the house.

Count Dracula came through the dark room like a black cloud.

"Quick!" cried Van Helsing. "We must get back! Now he has seen us, Mina may be in danger!"

My heart nearly stopped when I heard this. "Oh, Mina!" I cried silently. "I cannot lose Mina!"

But when we got back to Jack's house, everything was quiet. I ran upstairs. The bedroom door was locked. I called out to my friends. "Help me! Oh, help me!"

Together we broke down the door—and then my blood ran cold. A tall dark man was standing in the moonlight, by the window. In his arms he held my wife, my Mina! Her white nightdress had blood on it, and her face lay against Count Dracula. Blood dropped from his mouth, and he was holding Mina to him *while she drank his blood!*

I ran to her and tried to pull him away from her. Van Helsing ran at the Count and held up his gold cross.

When he saw the cross, Count Dracula moved back and dropped Mina's body. She gave a terrible cry and fell across the bed. A cloud moved across the moon, and when the moon came from behind it, Count Dracula was not there.

"Oh, Mina, my love!" I cried. I took her in my arms. "What has happened? Tell us!" I was wild with fear.

Mina shivered. "Don't leave me!" she cried. "Oh, please don't leave me!" Her face was pale, and we could see two little wounds on her neck. She put her head in her hands and gave a long, terrible scream. "Stay with me!" she cried.

And I held her in my arms until the first light of day showed in the east.

6
Dracula Must Die

The next day Van Helsing, Jack Seward, Arthur, and I made our plans. Mina was there too. She was very pale, but she wanted to help us. We knew that we had to kill Dracula before Mina died.

"If we don't," Van Helsing said, "Mina will die and will be a vampire for ever. I have been back to the Count's house this morning, and the last coffin has gone. We must find it. Count Dracula will be in it during the day. If we can find him before dark, we can kill him."

"But where is it now?" I asked wildly.

Of course, we did not know the answer. But then Mina spoke. "I feel that I am half a vampire already, and sometimes strange thoughts come into my head. I think that these thoughts are Count Dracula's. Just now, when you were speaking, I thought that I could hear the sound of a ship moving through water."

"Of course!" cried Van Helsing. "Dracula has decided to leave England! He knows now that we are his enemies and that it is dangerous for him here. So he is going back to Transylvania—by ship! We must find out which ships left for the Black Sea last night."

At the London shipping office we learned that one ship sailed for Varna in the Black Sea the night before. We also learned of a passenger who arrived at the last minute—a tall thin man in black. He had a pale face, burning eyes, and a very red mouth. And he had with him a long box!

"So," said Van Helsing. "The ship will take about three weeks to sail to Varna, but we will take the train across Europe and get there much faster. We leave tomorrow!"

We left London on a cold October day, and four days later we were in Varna. We made our plans and waited for the ship to arrive. Every day Mina told us that she could still hear the sound of water. But three weeks went by, and the ship did not arrive. Then, at last, we had news—the ship was not coming to Varna. It was already at Galatz!

We took the first train to Galatz, but we were too late. The box was no longer on the ship. "Someone came and took it this morning," one of the sailors told us.

We took the first train to Galatz, but we were too late.

We hurried back to our hotel to tell my dear Mina the news, but we saw that she knew it already, and her face was white with fear. "He has gone," she said quietly, "and he is taking me with him. Oh my dear friends! Before I change into a vampire, you must kill me! Then you must do what you did to poor Lucy, to give me rest. Tell me that you will do this for me!"

I held her hands, but I could not speak. If that day ever comes, I don't know how I will live through it.

Later, while Mina slept, we tried to make new plans.

"She is right," said Van Helsing unhappily. "Our poor Mina is in great danger. She is already beginning to change—her teeth are getting longer and sharper, and when the Count reads her thoughts, her eyes are hard and cold. We must find him and kill him—before it is too late!"

I can remember little of the next few days. I was wild with fear and anger. We learned that the Count's coffin was traveling by boat up the river, and Jack Seward, Arthur, and I began to follow in another boat. Van Helsing took my Mina with him in a carriage, and they began to drive across the mountains to Castle Dracula. When I said goodbye to her, my heart was breaking. Perhaps I will never see her again.

We followed the Count's boat for five days, but we could not catch it. Then we learned from some villagers that he was now traveling by road, so we bought horses and rode like the wind through the night.

By late afternoon on the next day, we were getting near to Castle Dracula. "We must ride faster!" I cried to the others. The sun was beginning to go down and then, suddenly, we saw on the road in front of us some men with a cart. And on the back of the cart was the coffin.

I had only one thought in my head—to kill the vampire, to finish him for ever. Arthur and Jack were right behind me when I got to the cart. I jumped from my horse onto the cart, and while Jack and Arthur fought the driver and the other men, I pushed the coffin to the ground. It fell and broke open. Count Dracula lay there, and the last light from the sun fell on his

terrible face. His eyes burned red and they looked at me in hate. In a few seconds, when the sun went down, he would be free to move. I jumped down to the ground, held my knife high over his heart, and brought it down as hard as I could. It went straight through the vampire's heart. Count Dracula gave a horrible scream, and then lay quiet. In the same second the sun went down, and when we looked into the coffin again, it was empty …

I jumped down to the ground, and held my knife high over his heart.

Above us on the hill was Castle Dracula, and soon we saw Van Helsing. He hurried down the hill to us, and my dear Mina was with him. I ran to her and took her in my arms. Her lovely face was bright and happy again. "It's all right, my love," she said softly. "We found the tombs of the three vampire women. They cannot hurt us now, and Dracula is dead at last! We can begin to live again."

"We can begin to live again."

GLOSSARY

become (past tense **became**) to change and begin to be something

believe to think that something is true

carriage a kind of "car" pulled by horses, for carrying people

cart a kind of open "car" pulled by horses, for carrying people or things

castle a big strong building that can keep enemies out

churchyard a place by a church where dead people lie under the ground

cloak a big loose coat, with no sleeves for the arms

coach a large kind of "car" pulled by horses, for carrying people

coffin a box in which a dead person lies

Count a title for a nobleman in some countries

curtain a piece of cloth that covers a window

earth dirt from the ground

fear (*n*) you feel this when you are afraid

frightened very afraid

garlic a plant with white flowers and a strong taste and smell, which is used in cooking

hammer (*n*) a heavy tool used for hitting things (e.g., nails into a wall)

hate (*n*) very strong dislike; opposite of "love"

heart the thing inside your chest, that pushes the blood around the body

hell the place where bad people go after they are dead

holy special because it is from the church

horrible very bad, terrible; making you very afraid or unhappy

howl (*v*) to make a long, loud crying sound

ice water that is hard because it is frozen (very cold)

kiss (*v*) to touch someone with your mouth to show love

lovely nice, beautiful

mirror a piece of glass where you can see yourself

pale with little color in the face

professor an important teacher at a university

servant someone who works in another person's house

sharp with an edge that cuts easily (e.g., a sharp knife)

shave to cut the hair off the face

shiver to shake with cold or fear

thought (*n*) something that you think

tomb a small stone building under or above the ground for a dead person

vampire the body of a dead person that comes alive at night and drinks the blood of living people

weak not strong

wolf a wild animal that looks like a dog

wound (*n*) a place on the body where something has cut or hurt you

Dracula

ACTIVITIES

ACTIVITIES

Before Reading

1 **Read the story introduction on the first page of the book and the back cover. How much do you know now about this story? Check one box for each sentence.**

	YES	NO
1 Count Dracula is a vampire.	☐	☐
2 He lives in a castle in England.	☐	☐
3 Jonathan Harker is going to marry Mina.	☐	☐
4 He is enjoying his stay in Castle Dracula.	☐	☐
5 He meets three beautiful women there.	☐	☐
6 Mina is also staying in Transylvania.	☐	☐
7 She gets lots of letters from Jonathan.	☐	☐
8 She is afraid that Dracula will hurt her.	☐	☐

2 **Can you guess what happens in this story? Use this table to make some sentences about your guesses.**

Jonathan Harker Count Dracula Mina Lucy	comes to England. goes to Transylvania. gets married. dies. nearly dies. becomes a vampire. kills somebody.

ACTIVITIES

While Reading

Read Chapters 1 and 2, (*Jonathan Harker's Diary*), and then answer these questions.

Why

1 ... didn't Jonathan want to go to Transylvania?
2 ... was Count Dracula pleased that his new house in England had a little church?
3 ... was Jonathan afraid when he looked in the mirror?
4 ... did the three women want to kiss Jonathan?
5 ... couldn't Jonathan leave the castle?
6 ... didn't Jonathan kill the Count in his coffin?
7 ... did Jonathan decide to escape?

Read Chapter 3 (*Mina's Story*). What did Mina see, hear, or do? Complete these sentences with words from the chapter.

1 At Whitby she heard about _____ which jumped off the strange ship from Varna.
2 She saw _____ behind Lucy in the churchyard.
3 Then she saw _____ on Lucy's neck.
4 She went _____ because Jonathan was ill there.
5 In Jonathan's diary she read about his _____.
6 She saw _____ in the streets of London.
7 In a letter from Arthur she heard that _____.

Before you read Chapter 4, can you guess the answers to these questions?

1 Will Arthur Holmwood find out why Lucy died?
2 What will happen to Lucy after her death?

Read Chapter 4, (*Jack Seward's Story*), and then answer these questions.

1 Who was Jack Seward?
2 What did Jack see on Lucy's neck?
3 Who was Professor Van Helsing?
4 What did Van Helsing say they must do?
5 Why weren't Arthur, Van Helsing, or Jack with Lucy on the night that Dracula came?
6 Why did Lucy ask Arthur to kiss her?
7 What happened to Lucy after her death?
8 What did Arthur have to do to Lucy?
9 What did the three men decide to do after that?

Before you read Chapters 5 and 6, can you guess what happens? Choose Y (yes) or N (no) for each sentence.

1 Van Helsing asks Jonathan and Mina to help. Y/N
2 The friends find Dracula in England and kill him. Y/N
3 Dracula catches one of the friends and drinks their blood. Y/N
4 One of them begins to change into a vampire. Y/N

5 One of them dies and becomes a vampire. Y/N
6 Dracula escapes, and the friends never find him. Y/N
7 Dracula kills two of the friends. Y/N
8 In the end one of the friends kills Dracula. Y/N

Read Chapters 5 and 6, (*Jonathan Harker's Diary*), and then join these halves of sentences.

1 Dracula's London house was full of coffins ...
2 On the night when the four men went out to put holy bread in Dracula's coffins, ...
3 Mina knew that Dracula was on a ship ...
4 The friends went by train to Varna, ...
5 Mina wanted her friends to kill her ...
6 Jonathan, Arthur, and Jack caught Dracula's cart in the mountains, ...
7 Jonathan pushed the coffin to the ground ...
8 When they looked into the coffin again, ...

9 before she changed into a vampire.
10 because she could hear his thoughts in her head.
11 it was empty.
12 Dracula found Mina alone in Jack Seward's house.
13 just before the sun went down.
14 but there they learned that Dracula's ship was at Galatz.
15 and drove his knife deep into Dracula's heart.
16 because he used them as daytime hiding places.

ACTIVITIES

After Reading

1 **What is a vampire? Complete the passage with these words from the story. (Use each word once.)**

become, bites, blood, bread, coffin, cross, day, dead, garlic, hammer, heart, ill, mirror, night, sharp, wood, wounds

A vampire is the body of a _____ person that drinks the
_____ of living people. If you look at a vampire in a _____,
you see nothing. During the _____ it lies quietly in its
_____, but at _____ it comes out and tries to catch people.
It has long _____ teeth, and it _____ into people's necks
and leaves two small _____ there. After a time the person
will get _____ and die and then _____ a vampire too.
You can frighten a vampire away if you wear a circle of
_____ flowers around your neck. Or you can hold a holy
_____ or put holy _____ in its coffin. The best way to kill
a vampire is to take a _____ and drive a long piece of
_____ through the vampire's _____.

2 **Now write a short description of Count Dracula. Use these notes to help you.**

- tall, thin / clothes / hair / face / mouth / teeth
- good English / address Castle Dracula / very dangerous

3 Here are some sentences from eight different letters in the story. Who wrote them, and to whom? Choose the right people from the list below. Then put the letters in the order in which they were written.

Arthur to Mina / *Jonathan to Mr. Hawkin*
Budapest Hospital to Mina / *Arthur to Dr. Jack Seward*
Jack to Professor Van Helsing / *Jonathan to Mina*
Jack and Van Helsing to Arthur / *Van Helsing to Jack*

1 ... and we are sorry to tell you that she is very weak. It won't be long now. Come as soon as you can.

2 ... The Count has asked me to stay here for another month. I hope that you will not need me in the office.

3 We have a young Englishman here, who has given us your name. He is still very ill and would like to see you, if you can make the journey from England ...

4 ... Don't forget—you must watch her all night! Don't leave her for a minute, or she'll be in great danger.

5 ... You helped me so much when I was your student. Now I need your help for a dear friend. Can you come?

6 I have some very sad news. You have lost a dear friend, and I have lost the girl I loved. It happened like this ...

7 ... You're my oldest friend, and also a doctor, so perhaps you can help her and find out why she is so ill.

8 My work in Transylvania is finished and I am coming home. I'm at Bistritz already and will see you soon ...

4 Here is a new illustration for the story. Find the best place in
the story to put the picture, and answer these questions.

The picture goes on page ____.

1 Who are the four characters in the picture?
2 What has just happened?
3 What happens next?

Now write a caption for the illustration.

Caption: _____

5 **Van Helsing has to tell Arthur that Lucy is a vampire. Put their conversation in the right order, and write in the speakers' names. Van Helsing speaks first (number 9).**

1 _____ "This *is* worse. Lucy was killed by a vampire, and she has now become a vampire herself."

2 _____ "Because Jack and I have seen her empty coffin. Come with us tonight, and we can show you."

3 _____ "How horrible! But it can't be Lucy! It can't be!"

4 _____ "What could be worse than my Lucy's death?"

5 _____ "I'm afraid it *is* possible. There is a vampire—a beautiful lady—who is catching small children at night. She bites their necks and drinks their blood."

6 _____ "It *is* her, Arthur. She leaves her tomb at night."

7 _____ "I can't believe this. I don't *want* to believe it. But I'll come with you and see for myself."

8 _____ "What! Lucy—a vampire? That's not possible!"

9 _____ "Arthur, I have something terrible to tell you."

10 _____ "How do you know she leaves her tomb?"

6 **What do you think about vampires? Do you agree (A) or disagree (D) with these ideas? Explain why.**

1 Stories about vampires are fun to read.

2 Nobody believes in vampires today.

3 It is more frightening to see a film about Dracula than to read a book about him.

ABOUT THE AUTHOR

Bram (short for Abraham) Stoker was born in Dublin, in Ireland, in 1847. After he finished his university studies there, he worked for the government, and married a Dublin girl, who had once nearly married Oscar Wilde. Like Wilde, Stoker was very interested in the theater, and in 1878 he moved to London, where he became the business manager of the famous actor, Sir Henry Irving. Together they ran the successful Lyceum Theatre in London. Stoker died in 1912.

His novel *Dracula* was published in 1897. There have been stories about vampires in eastern Europe for a very long time, and Stoker, who worked on his novel for four years, probably knew many of these stories. He himself said that the *Dracula* story came to him in a bad dream one night, after a large, rich dinner of crab meat. (This also happened to Robert Louis Stevenson, with his novel *Dr. Jekyll and Mr. Hyde*.)

Bram Stoker is often called "the least-known author of one of the best-known books." He wrote many other books, including horror stories such as *The Lair of the White Worm*, but it is because of *Dracula* that we remember him today. There have been many films about Count Dracula, and the book, which has never been out of print, is as popular today as it was a hundred years ago.

OXFORD BOOKWORMS LIBRARY

Classics • Crime & Mystery • Factfiles • Fantasy & Horror
Human Interest • Playscripts • Thriller & Adventure
True Stories • World Stories

The OXFORD BOOKWORMS LIBRARY provides enjoyable reading in English, with a wide range of classic and modern fiction, non-fiction, and plays. It includes original and adapted texts in seven carefully graded language stages which take learners from beginner to advanced level.

All Stage 1 titles, as well as over eighty other titles from Starter to Stage 6, are available as audio recordings. All Starters and many titles at Stages 1 to 4 are specially recommended for younger learners. Every Bookworm is illustrated, and Starters and Factfiles have full-color illustrations.

The OXFORD BOOKWORMS LIBRARY also offers extensive support. Each book contains an introduction to the story, notes about the author, a glossary, and activities. Additional resources include tests and worksheets, as well as answers for these and for the activities in the books. There is advice on running a class library, using audio recordings, and the many ways of using Oxford Bookworms in reading programs. Resource materials are available on the website <www.oup.com/elt/bookworms>.

The *Oxford Bookworms Collection* is a series for advanced learners. It consists of volumes of short stories by well-known authors, both classic and modern. Texts are not abridged or adapted in any way, but carefully selected to be accessible to the advanced student.

You can find details and a full list of titles in the *Oxford Bookworms Library Catalog* and *Oxford English Language Teaching Catalogs*, and on the website <www.oup.com/elt/bookworms>.

BOOKWORMS · CLASSICS · STAGE 2

Robinson Crusoe

DANIEL DEFOE

Retold by Diane Mowat

"I often walked along the shore, and one day I saw something in the sand. I went over to look at it more carefully … It was a footprint—the footprint of a man!"

In 1659 Robinson Crusoe was shipwrecked on a small island off the coast of South America. After fifteen years alone, he suddenly learns that there is another person on the island. But will this man be a friend—or an enemy?

BOOKWORMS · CLASSICS · STAGE 2

Huckleberry Finn

MARK TWAIN

Retold by Diane Mowat

Who wants to live in a house, wear clean clothes, be good, and go to school every day? Not young Huckleberry Finn, that's for sure.

So Huck runs away and is soon floating down the great Mississippi River on a raft. With him is Jim, a black slave who is also running away. But life is not always easy for the two friends.

And there's 300 dollars waiting for anyone who catches poor Jim …

BOOKWORMS · CRIME & MYSTERY · STAGE 2

Sherlock Holmes Short Stories

SIR ARTHUR CONAN DOYLE

Retold by Clare West

Sherlock Holmes is the greatest detective of them all. He sits in his room and smokes his pipe. He listens, watches, and thinks. He listens to the steps coming up the stairs; he watches the door opening—and he knows what question the stranger will ask.

In these three of his best stories, Holmes has three visitors to the famous apartment in Baker Street—visitors who bring their troubles to the only man in the world who can help them.

BOOKWORMS · HUMAN INTEREST · STAGE 2

New Yorkers

O. HENRY

Retold by Diane Mowat

A housewife, a tramp, a lawyer, a waitress, an actress—ordinary people living ordinary lives in New York at the beginning of this century. The city has changed greatly since that time, but its people are much the same. Some are rich, some are poor, some are happy, some are sad, some have found love, and some are looking for love.

O. Henry's famous short stories—sensitive, funny, sympathetic —give us vivid pictures of the everyday lives of these New Yorkers.

BOOKWORMS · FANTASY & HORROR · STAGE 3

Frankenstein

MARY SHELLEY

Retold by Patrick Nobes

Victor Frankenstein thinks he has found the secret of life. He takes parts from dead people and builds a new "man." But this monster is so big and frightening that everyone runs away from him—even Frankenstein himself!

The monster is like an enormous baby who needs love. But nobody gives him love, and soon he learns to hate. And, because he is so strong, the next thing he learns is how to kill ...

BOOKWORMS · CLASSICS · STAGE 3

A Christmas Carol

CHARLES DICKENS

Retold by Clare West

Christmas is humbug, Scrooge says just a time when you find yourself a year older and not a penny richer. The only thing that matters to Scrooge is business, and making money.

But on Christmas Eve three spirits come to visit him. They take him traveling on the wings of the night to see the shadows of Christmas past, present, and future—and Scrooge learns a lesson that he will never forget.